This Man
Bernardin

This Man
Bernardin

Photography of John H. White

Text by Eugene Kennedy

Preface by Joseph Cardinal Bernardin

Loyola Press

Loyola Press
3441 North Ashland Avenue
Chicago, Illinois 60657
All rights reserved
Printed in the United States of America

Library of Congress Cataloging-in-Publication Data
White, John H., 1945–
    This man Bernardin / photography of John H. White ; text by Eugene Kennedy.
        p.   cm.
    ISBN 0-8294-0909-2
    1. Bernardin, Joseph Louis, 1928–   . 2. Catholic Church-
-Illinois—Chicago Region—Bishops—Biography. 3. Cardinals-
-Illinois—Chicago Region—Biography. 4. Chicago Region (Ill.)-
-Biography. I. Kennedy, Eugene C. II. Title.
    BX4705.B38125W45 1996
    282'.092—dc20
    [B]   96-7997
                                             CIP

Frederick Falkenberg: art director
Jeremy Langford: managing editor, captions
Anne Marie Mastandrea: cover design, interior design
Jill Mark Salyards: production coordinator, interior design
Bob Masheris: photoshop work on dustjacket photographs and crest on p. viii
Robert Voights: map artwork on p. 180
Special thanks to Richard Cahan and Mark Jacob
Separations and printing: Gardner Lithograph, Buena Park, California
The Laser Fultone® process is a registered trademark of Gardner Lithograph

"To my dear friend Cardinal Bernardin,
Keep In Flight!"

—*John H. White*

Contents

AS THOSE WHO SERVE

Preface

I am aware from looking at these photographs how a shepherd can be viewed by his flock. He is at the center of so much attention, of course, not because of himself but because of what he symbolizes, because of the work God gives him to do. He is seen from this perspective, in good health and bad, on days of celebration and days of mourning, in times of crisis and times of tranquility. But he is in focus only as the shepherd in the fields is with his flock because he knows the way home and can be trusted to lead them safely on their journey.

This book appears to be about the watchful shepherd who is himself watched. For me, it is rather about the watching faithful whom I can see better in these photographs. It is therefore a book of revelation. The good people of Chicago, as well as other places, as unself-conscious in these scenes as they are in carrying out the ordinary duties of their lives, stand here filled with faith. That is the anchor of their lives and the motive that brings them to profess their beliefs publicly with their Archbishop. Their faces are filled with hope, not of a starry-eyed but of a realistic kind. These men and women have known every test of life, and one can see, on every page, that they have grown stronger through their patient bearing of these tests.

John White's photographs reveal truths about me, but more importantly they proclaim the deepest truth about the people of Chicago and elsewhere. They are a loving people who strive to live good lives, raise fine families, and serve their neighbors. They also give strength through their eyes to me, for, as I look into them, I feel the blessing of their acceptance, affection, and encouragement. They pray with me and for me as I do for them.

Let, then, the emphasis not be on the minister but on the ministry in which the people who line the sides and backgrounds of these photographs join me every day. Now we see in a glass, darkly, Saint Paul wrote about a mystery of faith. These pictures attest, however, that our common faith allows us *now* to see, even as we are seen, the saving goodness that radiates so gently from the faces of the believers who fill these pages.

Joseph Cardinal Bernardin

Introduction

This book is an assignment from God. It's a photographic mirror of Joseph Cardinal Bernardin, the beloved Archbishop of Chicago, whose hope, compassion, and kindness have enlightened the lives of his flock.

I first met Bernardin in 1979 in New York while I was covering Pope John Paul II's visit to the United States. The stranger who impressed me amidst the clamor of La Guardia Airport was then the Archbishop of Cincinnati.

There I was, a black photojournalist, the Protestant son of a Protestant minister and brother of three Protestant ministers. I had never heard of Bernardin, but his spirit was luminous. I recognized immediately what I have come to know more fully through our friendship: This man Bernardin is a lamplighter who ignites a flame in the hearts of those he meets.

During ceremonies marking his introduction to the Chicago faithful in 1982, the new shepherd stood before the crowd and said, with profound simplicity, "I am Joseph, your brother."

Though he doesn't billboard his authority and position, somehow one is compelled to hear everything he says. And each time, he offers spiritual recipes for daily living.

Over the years, I've turned on my photographic radar to capture private moments of this public man—from his quiet times of meditation to his precious visits with his ninety-one-year-old mother, Maria. What a blessing! Capturing this holy man from Italy's Dolomite Mountains to Chicago's overcrowded jails has given me a front-row seat to his life. He's granted me a personal passport to share his journey, which now allows me visually to present this man to the world.

This Man Bernardin has been a labor of love. The images were captured with my Nikon 35-mm cameras on Tri-X black-and-white film—with the exception of the old family photos—and I hand-printed each photo for this book.

I've seen the Cardinal electrify throngs of thousands. I've seen him cry silent tears at a funeral. I've seen him work as a bridge builder during troubled times. I've observed him as a simple Christian servant. In this project I share the eye of my camera, and the eye of my soul.

I am thankful for the gift of photography. I am most grateful to the *Chicago Sun-Times* for permission to use a few of the pictures I took during assignments. I'm also thankful to the Archdiocese of Chicago and to Loyola Press for being the vehicle that has helped me accomplish my dreams. To my special friends who shared their particular talents, I extend my heartfelt thanks. But most of all, I thank God, who assigned this project to me and who willed this task of documenting the life of Joseph Cardinal Bernardin. This project reflects what I've learned about Bernardin's spiritual walk and his intimacy with God.

So, if a little child were to ask me, "Picture man, who is this man, Bernardin?" I would simply say, "He is a gentle, caring priest who loves God and people, and seeks to serve both."

1
Private Moments

"Private moments for me are really prayer moments. Whether reading a book, writing a speech, listening to music, or simply relaxing, I enjoy being alone with my thoughts. It is in those moments when we are alone that we enter into a much deeper understanding of ourselves and our relationship with the Lord. My personal time is usually spent in the early hours of the morning. I begin each day in prayer, which includes the Liturgy of the Hours, the rosary, and meditation. Then I celebrate the Eucharist. I find that I become rather empty if I don't have that kind of spiritual nourishment at the beginning of the day. Through prayer I become grounded in the Lord, which has a positive effect on the way I view the events of my life and make decisions. I am very much convinced of this. When people ask me about prayer, I put a very high priority on personal prayer. It can take different forms for different people. And I do not in any way deemphasize the importance of public prayer. But I believe that if we are well nourished by our private prayer, then we are better prepared to engage in the public prayer of the church."

One of Cardinal Bernardin's favorite places for quiet time and personal reflection is in the library of his residence on North State Parkway on Chicago's North Side.

In what space would we look to find Joseph Cardinal Bernardin?

Space is a word as plain and hard as the streets of the Cardinal's Depression-era boyhood in Columbia, South Carolina. Yet the word is rich, complex, and not without mystery, much as Cardinal Bernardin's own journey ever since that lost and gone time.

Space evokes the vast envelope of galaxies beyond ourselves and beyond our reach. It also refers to the limitless spiritual depths within us that are in our keeping. Space suggests something as secular as the curb where you can park or as sacred as the reaches of a cathedral where you may pray. It summons up a door opening on opportunity or one closing in restriction, a sphere of privacy or a market of public display, the comfortable place called home where you return changed by facing the dangerous world. Space may be time bound tightly as a scroll or time broken open in eternity. Cardinal Bernardin's pilgrimage has taken him through all these spaces.

The world imagines the Midwest as space, that region beyond the map's first fold that widens and stretches into prairie the eye strains to measure. This is America, visitors say, this place where the philosopher's elements intermingle: the fertile black earth and the unending sky, the water of the glacial lakes, and the man-made fire of big cities and blast furnaces.

Chicago was born of these forces, and its space has always tingled with their energies. For Chicago is the classic American space of contradiction and mystery. Now a brawler and now a patron of the arts, the city makes a stranger welcome but makes demands as well. Any man appointed to be Chicago's Catholic Archbishop is automatically granted an honored place at its civic, cultural, and political tables. But sideways and knowing glances measure him: Will the newcomer fit into the prescribed dimensions of a traditional role or carve out a place of his own?

The Archdiocese of Chicago was a troubled space when Joseph Louis Bernardin, just past his fifty-fourth birthday, was transferred from Cincinnati to become its Archbishop in the summer of 1982. His predecessor, John

Patrick Cody, had died in his sleep in April, his body wasted by illness and his spirit worn down by a year of accusations of questionable financial practices, for which evidence was never produced. The boundaries of the old Cardinal's life had been shrunk by the astringent publicity and, in the December before he died, he passed his fiftieth ordination anniversary as a sovereign under siege might, in the sheltered space of the archdiocesan seminary in Mundelein instead of in the city itself.

So quiet and untended were its grounds, so few the lights seen at night that people wondered whether Cody was still living in the Archbishop's red-bricked official residence built in 1885 on the edge of Lincoln Park. Its handsomely paneled rooms converted into office space by its solitary resident, the structure symbolized the Archdiocese—a once-great vessel now aimlessly adrift.

Bernardin, who was named a Cardinal just four months after coming to Chicago, brought his own life into the residence, restoring the simplicity of its traditional rooms, healing its aching emptiness by making it a home for other priests to live with him, fashioning a community for prayer and Mass in the small chapel. Three nuns joined him to maintain the house and prepare the meals. The grounds were cleared and tended. Flowers bloomed again in the yard, and guests climbed the old steps beneath the porte cochere to share the hospitality of the church and its Archbishop.

As the decaying house had groaned inwardly with the isolation and misunderstanding of its former occupant's last years, it now hummed with activity. Bernardin had made the space his own. His possessions— his family pictures, the books and paintings he had chosen throughout his career, the gifts that spoke to him of their donors, the way he arranged his desk, the careful way he worked—suddenly brought so much warmth of human association into the residence's space that people were hard pressed to remember how lonely and quiet it had been before.

Collar open and deep in thought, Cardinal Bernardin works at his desk at his residence. There he prepares his speeches, homilies, and other important papers.

(Left) The Cardinal's office at the residence reveals simple elegance and order.

(Above) The "Dove of Peace" was given to Cardinal Bernardin in 1983 by Ms. Helen Boehm and the Showcase at Wheeling Nursery in honor of his work as chairman of the committee that drafted the Catholic Bishops' Pastoral Letter "The Challenge of Peace: God's Challenge and Our Response."

(Left) Of the many awards, gifts, and mementos dear to the Cardinal, the Laetare Medal from the University of Notre Dame is one of his most cherished (*hanging in miniature bell jar*). Bernardin is only the second prelate—next to the late John Cardinal Dearden of Detroit—to receive the distinguished award for outstanding contributions to American Catholic life.

5

Cardinal Bernardin's gold ring is a symbol of his authority and his responsibility. It was given to him by Pope John Paul II when Bernardin became a cardinal in 1983. All of those appointed as cardinals by Pope John Paul II receive the same ring, which bears the image of Mary and Saint John at the Crucifixion.

(*Left*) Even for Cardinal Bernardin, life's road is paved with paperwork.

(*Below*) The Cardinal reads from the Liturgy of the Hours each day. He says, "The Liturgy of the Hours comes in four volumes for the seasons of the liturgical year. I have worn out several sets over the past forty-five years."

The residence of the Archbishop of Chicago has anchored the southeast corner of North State Parkway and North Avenue since 1885. The house has seventeen chimneys.

(*Right*) Cardinal Bernardin adjusts his cuff links as he makes his way down to the chapel on the first floor of the residence to celebrate the Eucharist.

Lending a helping hand in the kitchen is nothing new to Cardinal Bernardin. He recalls, "When I was growing up, after my father died, my mother taught me how to get supper started so that when she came home from work she could finish it and share the evening meal with my sister and me." Here he stirs soup and cuts bread while Sister Mary Lucia Skalka prepares chicken in the kitchen. "He eats everything," she says, "but Italian food is his favorite."

During Mass in the residence chapel, Cardinal Bernardin is immersed in prayer.

(*Right*) The Cardinal takes a moment to pray for his personal intentions during Mass at Little Sisters of the Poor. "Through prayer I become more connected with the Lord, whom I serve as a bishop and a shepherd. For the most part I pray for others, but I do include myself," says the Cardinal. "I pray for the Archdiocese, especially for the priests and those they serve. I also pray for the strength and intelligence to handle the challenges of each day."

An avid reader, Cardinal Bernardin enjoys history, biographies, and books on Christology. He also subscribes to and reads many journals, both religious and secular.

(*Left*) The Cardinal enjoys the warm sunlight as he reads near one of the windows on the second floor of his home.

2
Family

"My family has always been very important to me. When my parents emigrated from Italy to America in 1927, they brought with them three essential qualities: respect for hard work, deep faith in God, and commitment to family life. During our years together in Columbia, South Carolina, my parents taught my sister, Elaine, and me the importance of having a solid work ethic. They also made sure that we went to church together on Sunday as a family.

"After my father died of cancer when I was six and Elaine was two, my mother got a job as a seamstress and took care of us. She became both mother and father. She has always been a strong woman and an enormous part of my life. Early on, my mother taught my sister and me to deeply treasure our family by telling us stories of our relatives back in Italy. When the three of us were finally able to visit Italy together in 1957, I got a chance to see firsthand the close-knit families of relatives she had always described. I immediately felt at home, and have ever since. I am very grateful for all the joy and support my family has given me throughout the years."

A proud mother and her dutiful son pose for their annual Christmas photograph in 1991 at Little Sisters of the Poor, where Maria Bernardin makes her home. The picture has become a holiday tradition. The Cardinal always rushes to send copies to his family.

The white-robed monks of the Dolomite Mountains stand in silent choir above the slopes and plains of northern Italy, binding them eternally to the sky. They peer into every window of Tonadico di Primiero, a village so close to the border that its citizens think themselves Austrian even as they speak Italian. The town's glistening white homes and buildings, including the nearly five-century-old Saint Sebastian's Church, are rooted like ancient teeth in the soil. Inspecting the church register after becoming a cardinal, Joseph Bernardin's hand stopped at the space filled by old-fashioned script to note that his mother, Maria Maddalena Simion, had been born there almost eighty years before.

The new Cardinal's father, Joseph, along with his five brothers, apprenticed themselves to the ageless mountains, working their sugar-white marble facings until they became master stonecutters. In the town far below, Maria Simion discovered her gift for the finest sewing. Mystery flowed off these mountains, vesting the ordinary mysteries of village life with their own majesty: those of hard work from first light until last, of the milestones of family life, the births and weddings, the days for feasting and the days for mourning. The rumble of the Great War spread across the valley, calling young men, including Joseph, into the army even as God's voice in the people's needs called Maria's oldest brother, Pietro, into the priesthood.

In this Old World setting, the sturdy young stonecutter and the beautiful black-haired seamstress entered into an old-fashioned romance. For all its transcendent wonder, they discovered that love is also a space of unexpected mystery, of wanting to be together and finding they must be apart, of experiencing flashes of eternity and feeling the full burden of time, days in the desert when, longing to do something, humans find that there is nothing to do but wait. The young lovers came to know all of these, enduring delays patiently so that it could finally be said of them what was written biblically of Isaac and Rachel, that "the years passed as one day because of the greatness of their love."

They needed the depth of their sustaining affection when Joseph traveled with his brothers to the New World, its twenties boom increasing the demand for artisans to cut the marble to clad the walls of its banks and mansions. He and a brother who was betrothed to one of Maria's sisters finally settled in Columbia, South Carolina. They rented a home on Wayne Street where they hoped to bring their future wives within a few years.

But mystery now fell like a distorted shadow across the young couple's lives. Returning to Italy, Joseph complained of health problems that doctors eventually diagnosed as cancer. Across the space of the years, we can see the earnest stonecutter father in his son the Cardinal, for, after surgery, Joseph insisted that Maria speak to the doctors so she could hear for herself reassurances that, after so many interruptions, they could marry in Tonadico in 1927 and travel to America where life would finally begin for them.

But their interval of happiness was to be brief. The son, Joseph, born to them on April 2, 1928, was barely four and Maria was pregnant with the daughter who would be called Elaine when the father's illness returned. Life that had once bubbled in the little home now slowed, as indeed it did across the Depression-stricken country. The sense of spontaneous happiness and largeness of opportunity was being squeezed out of America. The range of life narrowed in the house where, through months of slowly declining hope, Maria kept vigil at the bedside of her dying husband.

Joseph Bernardin, known as Beppi, died as the economy turned hope into hardscrabble across the South. Maria decided not to touch the $5,000 estate but to husband it so she could build a house later on. She did not feel sorry for herself but earned her way with her fingers as a seamstress both at home and for the Works Progress Administration, raising her children and drawing from the deep well of the faith that had nourished her life. Joseph, who entered the public school at five and who often fixed family meals and cared for his sister, grew up in a place where the wounds of the Civil War had not fully healed. The space of his childhood was hardened and shrunken by the Depression, forcing his generation to make passage across it on a diet of duty and obligation.

The Cardinal's mother, Maria Bernardin, displays her joyous smile.

(*Left*) Tracing his roots, Cardinal Bernardin finds his mother's baptismal record in the 490-year-old Church of Saint Sebastian in the tiny Italian village of Tonadico di Primiero, where both of his parents were born.

(*Above*) Giuseppi (Joseph) Bernardin, known as Beppi, was a stonecutter who served as a sergeant in the Austro-Hungarian Army before he married Maria Simion (*top left*).

(*Left*) This photograph, taken around 1924, shows Maria, second from right in the back row, with her family. Maria's parents, Giovanni and Giuseppina Simion, sit on either side of their son, Pietro, a newly ordained priest. The others are Maria's sisters and brothers.

Maria and Joseph posed for a portrait on their wedding day in Tonadico di Primiero in 1927. Soon after Maria and Joseph married, they left their Italian home and immigrated to the New World, settling in Columbia, South Carolina.

In remembering his father, who died in 1934, Cardinal Bernardin says, "I'm told that my father was a great reconciler, that he didn't like conflicts and always tried to bring people together. When people tell me I have similar traits, I know it is because of my father. I do remember his great love for Elaine and me, especially when he was very ill and his future looked bleak. One example of my father's love that will forever stand out in my mind happened when I was about four. It was summer and our family was visiting friends. My father had recently undergone cancer-related surgery on his left shoulder, and he was wearing a bandage under a white short-sleeved shirt. During the day I had been sitting on a metal railing on the porch of our friends' home when suddenly I fell backwards, hit the ground, and started crying. My father immediately jumped the rail and picked me up. As he held me in his arms, I could see blood soaking through his shirt where he'd had the surgery. But he paid no attention to himself; he wanted to make sure I was all right."

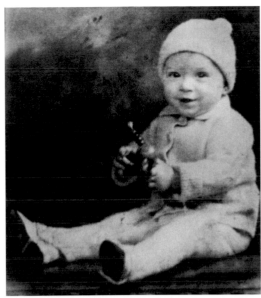

On April 2, 1928, the recently married couple had their first child, a son, and named him Joseph. Here young Joseph is shown at eight months (*below*) and at one year (*left*).

(*Far left*) In the only photograph of the Bernardin family together, Joseph and his mother, father, and newly arrived sister, Elaine, pose in front of their home in South Carolina in 1932.

(*Above*) Joseph and Elaine smile for a studio portrait taken in 1938.

(*Left*) Elaine, whose married name is Addison, still lives in Columbia, South Carolina.

"My sister and I are very close," says the Cardinal. "We spent a great deal of time together as kids because I looked after her when my mother was working. I remember the pastor of our parish wanted my sister and me to attend the Catholic elementary school, which was one mile away. My mother, who also wanted us to go there, said that we would have to wait until I was old enough to take care of myself and my sister. So, when I reached the fourth grade, we were enrolled in the Catholic school and I walked with my sister to and from class each day. We got to be good friends during those years."

A twenty-three-year-old Joseph Bernardin (*second from left*) shares some fun with fellow seminarians at Saint Mary's Catechetical Camp near Beaufort, South Carolina, in 1951. He was more serious when his mother came to visit (*right*).

Before entering the seminary, Cardinal Bernardin had earned a scholarship to the University of South Carolina, where, after his first year, he planned on entering the pre-med program. During the summer following his freshman year, however, a couple of young priests from his hometown parish took a great interest in the budding student and talked with him about entering the priesthood. "The tactic they used," recalls Bernardin, "was to show me that my interest in being a physician indicated that I wanted to help people, to reach out to others. They told me I could do that as a priest. So, almost overnight I decided to try the seminary. My mother was very concerned I'd lose my scholarship and have nothing to fall back on if I didn't like the seminary. But I went and liked it very much."

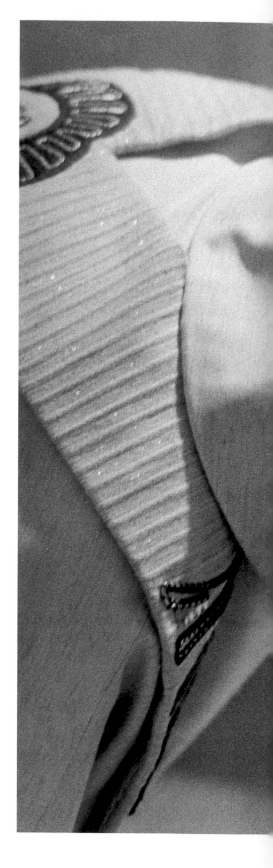

Throughout his journey from seminarian to cardinal, Joseph Bernardin and his mother have shared a special relationship. The Cardinal greets his mother every day with a simple kiss.

The Cardinal hosts a small birthday luncheon for his mother each year at the residence. (*Below right*) Sister Barbara Charles, who died in 1995, looks on as the Cardinal shares a gift with his mother.

The home of the Little Sisters of the Poor, in Chicago's Lincoln Park neighborhood, is the setting for the Cardinal's daily visits with his mother. Each year the Cardinal celebrates Christmas Eve Mass in the chapel. Maria has long held the role of carrying the baby Jesus to the Nativity scene.

On September 18, 1983, Joseph Cardinal Bernardin celebrated Mass in his parents' hometown of Tonadico di Primiero. His first visit as a "prince of the church" was marked by warm sun, crisp air, and a joyful celebration. Wearing a cardinal's choir robes and skullcap, Bernardin led a procession through the streets to the Church of Saint Sebastian. Earlier he was officially welcomed by Gianfranco Gadenz, president of the valley of Tonadico, who hailed Bernardin as "a son of our land, one of us, who is a witness to the values that make big our little village."

Before a standing-room-only congregation of hundreds of worshippers, Cardinal Bernardin celebrated Mass with relatives and friends in the dimly lit church that glowed in love that day. A handmade sign in front of the altar celebrated the Cardinal's connection to his roots with these simple words: "The altar which saw your parents married sees you today as a cardinal."

Giuseppe Ploner was the husband of a first cousin, Monica Ploner, on Cardinal Bernardin's father's side.

(*Top right*) Cardinal Bernardin's maternal uncle Vittorio Simion with his wife, Giuseppina.

(*Middle right*) With the Cardinal (*second from left*) during one of his visits to Tonadico are three first cousins on his father's side: (*from left*) Agostino Zagonel, Gaspare Zagonel, and Giacomo Zagonel. The cheeses they are holding were made from the milk of cows that graze in the summer months high in the mountains that surround the village.

(*Bottom right*) The Cardinal signs pictures and cards for those who want a memento of his visit with them.

Framed by nature's beauty, Cardinal Bernardin poses with some of his young relatives.

(*Left*) Tonadico di Primiero is nestled in a deep valley in the Dolomite Mountains in northern Italy.

(*Following pages*) The tourist beams with pride in his family's native land.

A cowherd drives his cattle down from the high pastures and through the streets of Tonadico as part of a parade that ushers in the winter season (*left*). Cows are adorned with headdresses for the celebration (*above*), and the bells around their necks (*top*) mix with the chimes of the church bells in the mountain air.

"When I first drove into the valley of Primiero as a young man," recalls Cardinal Bernardin, "it was as if I'd been there before. My mother kept a photo album that she had brought with her when she came to America. She used to go through it with me and tell stories of the people and places on each page. Later on I would flip through the album myself and study the faces, as well as the houses and surrounding mountains. So, I felt very at home during my first visit to Tonadico, which is one of the villages of the valley of Primiero. Every time I go back I feel at home."

3

Chicago's New Archbishop

"If God gives me strength and grace, I shall preside in charity over the Church in Chicago from the bishop's chair of this cathedral for many years. When, in the year of my retirement, the Archbishop's crozier is passed to my successor, we shall have reached the year two thousand plus three. A sobering thought for me and for you as well. Together we may cross the threshold of the third millennium, a milestone for civilization and for Christianity. For however many years I am given, I give myself to you. I offer you my service and leadership, my energies, my gifts, my mind, my heart, my strength, and, yes, my limitations. I offer you myself in faith, hope, and love."

[Most Reverend Joseph L. Bernardin, Homily for Liturgy of Solemn Installation of the Seventh Archbishop of Chicago, Holy Name Cathedral, August 25, 1982]

Four days after his formal installation as the seventh Archbishop of Chicago, Joseph Bernardin held a Mass of greeting and thanksgiving in Grant Park for the people of the Archdiocese.

"Make no small plans," the great architect Daniel Burnham had urged of Chicago's projected urban design, capturing the largeness of the city's ambition. Chicago teethed on the bone of its own contradictions. No place could so easily encompass and yet differentiate the sacred and the profane. Chicago needed room for both the fine arts and the manly arts, to be ballet dancer and Sumo wrestler, to accommodate the patrons of Orchestra Hall and the protégés of City Hall, to be something beyond the reach of European-flavored New York or Oriental-laced Los Angeles, unmistakably and unapologetically itself, the true American place.

How, the politicians, financiers, and plain people wondered as they gathered for his installation, would Joseph L. Bernardin, this son of Italian immigrants called out of the deep South by way of assignments in Washington and Cincinnati, fill the archbishop's prominent place in Chicago's life? The Pope's representative, Archbishop Pio Laghi, emphasized Chicago's depth and breadth as he read the official documents in Holy Name Cathedral afloat with summer light on the feast of Saint Louis in August 1982. He inflected the Latin word *maxima* as a sommelier might the name of a prize vintage: *maxima*, "the greatest" of Catholic archdioceses. Chicago sat at the center of both the United States and the vast structure of the Roman Catholic Church.

Few people have found themselves in such sharp focus at that point between chapters of history where expectation is everything. In the murky space far above the cathedral sanctuary hung the tasseled cardinalatial ceremonial hats of dead archbishops, hoisted there to disintegrate as symbols of the shortness of time and the smallness of the space allotted to even the most powerful of prelates. Bernardin was well aware of these reminders as he preached for the first time to the governor, the mayor, the bank and business presidents who looked up politely but appraisingly at the new Archbishop.

The new Archbishop had already met with his priests whose morale had suffered during Cardinal Cody's last illness-ridden years. The Archdiocese, once the dynamic center of innovation in pastoral and liturgical matters, had found its energies stymied and its creativity dulled during that purgatorial era. Now, every hope of renewal and revitalization was placed in Joseph Bernardin. So, too, the thousands of Catholics who had once participated actively in programs that ranged from marriage preparation to the search for social justice and racial equality longed, as generations in the Bible did, for a redemptive sign.

Bernardin understood that many priests and people wanted him to do something dramatic, to claim a place of prominence on the stage of Chicago's civic and ecclesiastical life. Some leaders, he knew, would respond by filling the long-aching void with heroic words or decrees that, like a biblical amnesty, would free everyone of past sins and memories or give reassurance that a prophet had arrived to lead them safely out of the wilderness.

Instead, Bernardin, knowing that he risked disappointing some, presented himself as he was, an archbishop ready for his record to be written in public, whose measured gestures were not theatrical but filled the space he framed so carefully with his hands as he emphasized a point. He could not save the priests by changing their lives but he dedicated himself to working with them as they revived themselves. He had not come as a protective father but as "Joseph, your brother." Bernardin worried less about the size of the place he had to occupy than about putting the fullness of himself into it. He wanted to sink foundations deep but in plain sight for a church that could survive into the next century.

After the necessarily restricted official welcoming, the new Archbishop asked for a day on which he could celebrate Mass for all the people in a place where he could then meet and mingle with them. In the Gospel, great and small miracles take place at the water's edge. Bernardin had not come to work miracles on Lake Michigan but to make room around himself, as the democracy of seasides allows, for everyone to see him and to symbolize with him what no prelate could any longer symbolize only by himself, the mystery of the Church as a people called to serve, rather than an institution out to dominate, Chicago.

Under the watchful eye of the Chicago skyline, newly installed Archbishop Bernardin shared his joy and enthusiasm with a sea of well-wishers during the Mass in Grant Park. His message then remains the same today: "The portion of this great Christian, Catholic family which is the Archdiocese of Chicago is . . . an extended family that encompasses the most diverse members: priests, deacons, religious, and laity; Black, White, Hispanic, and Oriental; rural, suburban, and urban; parishes, hospitals, schools, universities, administrative offices; parents and children, childless couples, the single, the widowed, the separated, the divorced; those who give all of their energies to the Church and those who are all but inactive. Today we celebrate the unity of us all."

(*Following pages*) Welcoming waves. Cardinal Bernardin and the people of Chicago exchange warm greetings in the summer afternoon.

A reverent Archbishop Bernardin consecrates the Host during the most sacred moment of the Mass and distributes Communion to disabled members of the Archdiocese.

A rainbow of people turned out to greet the new shepherd. This fence was no obstacle for little eyes as they took in the events of the day.

"I was overwhelmed by the turnout at the Grant Park Mass," says Cardinal Bernardin. "I came up with the idea for the Mass on the plane from Cincinnati to Chicago a few days after the appointment was announced to make arrangements for the installation. I was trying to think of a place where the people of Chicago and I could greet each other. I knew the cathedral was too small to house everyone, so I asked Mayor Jane Byrne if we could use Grant Park for a picnic Mass. She liked the idea, and it turned out to be a great day."

The August 25, 1982, Mass at Holy Name Cathedral marked the formal installation of Joseph L. Bernardin as Archbishop of Chicago and attracted many of the city's prominent players. Those present included Mayor Jane Byrne (*middle*); Governor James R. Thompson (*top right*); and Eleanor "Sis" Daley (*bottom right*), the widow of the late Mayor Richard J. Daley.

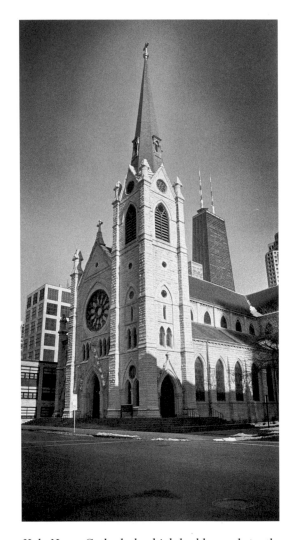

Holy Name Cathedral, which had been elegantly restored during the late 1960s, provided a dramatic setting for the installation of Archbishop Bernardin, who led the procession up the steps and into the church.

4

The Leader

"One of the things I wanted to do when I arrived was establish a calmer climate in the Chicago church . . . and I think that has happened. . . . I also wanted to facilitate greater involvement on the part of the priests, religious, and laity in the overall life of the archdiocese. That includes participating in the decision-making process and the development of policy, and I see signs that this is happening, slowly but surely. Some examples of my efforts in this direction include the Archdiocesan Pastoral Council, the Consejo Pastoral Hispano Arquidiocesano, the Presbyteral Council, the College of Archdiocesan Consultors, and the Finance Council. . . . Other programs I feel have really contributed to the quality of life in the archdiocese include Catholic education in its many forms; the Big Shoulders Fund, which helps support the inner-city schools; the Center for Development in Ministry; the Catholic Health Alliance of Metropolitan Chicago, and, of course, Catholic Charities. . . ."

[Joseph Cardinal Bernardin, from an interview on the occasion of his tenth anniversary as Archbishop of Chicago, *The New World,* August 21, 1992]

The Cardinal meets with members of the Religious Leaders of Metropolitan Chicago, an ecumenical group of Catholics, Protestants, and Jews.

Being named Archbishop of Chicago granted Joseph Bernardin the first place at the table of American ecclesiastical power. He was not naive or uninstructed about both his potential influence and his very real responsibilities. He consciously chose to lead not from an elevated throne but by standing on the same plane with his people; not by beribboned decrees but through building consensus; not from behind the gold filigreed doors of the clerical universe but, as at his initial Grant Park Mass, in the open and from the very middle of the men and women who constituted the local Church of Chicago.

He led by instinct, by inheritance, and through all that he had learned in long apprenticeships with Archbishop Paul Hallinan of Atlanta and Detroit's John Cardinal Dearden, who had been the first president of the newly recognized National Conference of Catholic Bishops following the Second Vatican Council. In these men Bernardin discovered fathers who, in their warmth, integrity, and vision, blended in memory with his own father. These mentors reinforced his sense that the sun of history

had set on the British and the ecclesiastical empires and that bishops could no longer function as viceroys in a vast clerical raj. Vatican II had called the Church back to its beginnings, asking it to forsake its monarchical vesture. Pope Paul VI symbolized this movement when he retired the crown-like papal tiara and radically simplified the robes and privileges of once-princely cardinals. Bishops were expected to lead not as commanders but as servants.

Archbishop Bernardin followed this path intuitively, naturally, unsensationally. Priests and people soon recognized that, even though he chose to fill it differently, he valued and did not reject the place earlier archbishops had struggled to establish and maintain for the once-predominantly immigrant Catholic people of Chicago. He would not sound a note false to his own character by selling the Archbishop's residence, as some enthusiastic Catholics had proposed. Nor would he sell the seminary complex that, in its collections and structures, resembled San Simeon as much as its builder, George Cardinal Mundelein, resembled William

Randolph Hearst as a master of public power and conspicuous consumption. Bernardin appreciated all that his predecessors had done on behalf of past generations of mostly poor Catholics who took heart from and would accept nothing less than their archbishop living in a house as big as the governor's. Bernardin wrote his own signature across this many-layered Chicago inheritance by transforming its properties into vehicles of a servant rather than a magisterial church.

Yet something deeper than wisdom—personal grace and good manners—emerged as slowly and truly as a photographic image in development. Bernardin cocked his head gently like a confessor who could not be shocked by anything he heard. He listened, steepling his expressive hands, pursing his lips and pausing before he spoke to ensure that others had their say. He selected the role of tireless mediator determined to draw the best out of both sides before coming to a decision. Lacking affectation, he was always himself, hearing people out long after someone else would have made excuses and extinguished the lights. Bernardin was always prepared; he must have been good at homework when he was a little boy back in South Carolina, where the knowledge of death and the duty of being grown-up were thrust upon him before due time.

That undefensive and unpretentious person could be seen in the newly named Cardinal who, unlike George Cardinal Mundelein who had been chauffeured by a uniformed driver in a limousine with crimson-strutted wheels, drove his own sedan throughout the Archdiocese. His most prominent characteristics—consistency, reliability, and trustworthiness—coalesced into one. Chicago embraced a good son and recognized in his invalid mother the woman who had given him her best gifts: faith grounded in reality, an earthy and forgiving spirituality, gravity of purpose suffused with good humor, a modest sense of himself. He seemed never to forget what Maria Maddalena Simion had whispered to him on the day when, at age thirty-eight, he was first made a bishop: "Stand up and walk straight and try not to look too pleased with yourself."

As the spiritual leader of more than two million Catholics in the Archdiocese of Chicago, Cardinal Bernardin is a bridge builder with a brilliant mind and a gentle touch.

The Cardinal announces grand plans for the sesquicentennial celebration of the Archdiocese of Chicago in 1993. Appropriately, he commenced the festivities from Old Saint Patrick's, the city's oldest church and public building, located at 122 South Desplaines Street.

(*Left*) Many who have met Cardinal Bernardin have been moved by his gentle manner and his gift for listening.

As the leader of Chicago's Catholic community, Cardinal Bernardin endorses a campaign against drugs spearheaded by the Reverend Michael Pfleger (*seated beside Bernardin*). Bernardin's support attracted close to fifty priests from all over the city to this press conference in 1989.

The Cardinal has always maintained a
close relationship with the city's mayors.
Here he shares a laugh with Mayor
Harold Washington (*above*) and a
handshake with Mayor Richard M. Daley.

Eye-to-eye, heart-to-heart, the Cardinal greets young friends at Our Lady of Grace Church, 2446 North Ridgeway. Bernardin is responsible for the largest parochial school system (and the eleventh-largest school system of any kind, public or private) in the United States.

Cardinal Bernardin has always placed a priority on the importance of education and says, "I am proud of the work we do in our inner-city schools, and I work hard to keep them open. We have some forty thousand children in our inner-city schools, 40 percent of whom are not Catholic. I started the Big Shoulders Fund to raise needed money for these schools. Each year it takes a lot of work to keep these schools going, as well as the Fund. I am happy to say that we have been quite successful."

Cardinal Bernardin is serenaded by folksingers at Saint Mark's Church, 1048 North Campbell Avenue.

(*Right*) With a tender touch, the Cardinal bends to greet young parishioners on their own level. Here he is at Holy Angels Church, 607 East Oakwood Boulevard, the largest parochial African-American elementary school in the United States.

Cardinal Bernardin has found the faith and the will to make tough decisions. Faced with a $14-million deficit in 1990, Bernardin initiated drastic cost-cutting measures throughout the Archdiocese of Chicago. He closed 33 of 415 parishes and 18 of 384 schools that year alone. "Closing and consolidating were not signs that the Archdiocese was dying. They were instead an acknowledgment that changes had to take place to better utilize our limited resources," he says. "What was most unfortunate was having to do so much of it at one time." As of 1996, there are 377 parishes and 295 schools. At the end of the fiscal year 1995 the Archdiocese had a surplus of $13 million.

(*Above and left*) Cardinal Bernardin drives himself whenever he can to his many appointments. Here he arrives without fanfare at Saint Mark's Church, notes in hand, and is greeted by friendly children.

(*Top*) Room for one more? The watchful Cardinal paid close attention in 1990 as children tried out their new playground at the Academy of Saint Benedict the African, 6547 South Stewart Avenue.

The Cardinal leads the way after
a meeting at the University of
Saint Mary of the Lake, in north
suburban Mundelein. The guest
of honor on this occasion was
Basil Cardinal Hume, Archbishop
of Westminister in England
(*front row, far right*).

The Cardinal meets with ecumenical leaders at Saint James Episcopal Cathedral, 65 East Huron Street. In a 1989 pastoral letter, Bernardin wrote, "We need to speak, and, with equal attention, we need to listen. The structures already in place for ecumenical and interfaith dialogue and cooperation must be sustained and strengthened."

(*Left*) During one of his many visits to Italy, Cardinal Bernardin speaks with Archbishop Giovanni Gottardi of Trent. The Cardinal maintains relationships with many prelates of other countries.

(*Following pages*) Even during a short recess, the Cardinal keeps working at a 1987 meeting at the Center for Development in Ministry in suburban Mundelein.

(*Far left*) As fire consumed Holy Angels Church on June 9, 1986, the cross stayed atop the structure until the very end.

(*Above*) Rebuilding efforts at Holy Angels began immediately, and Cardinal Bernardin shared his support along with (*front row, left to right*) Alderman Timothy Evans, Father George Clements, and (*second row, left to right*) Alderman Bobby Rush and Mayor Harold Washington.

(*Left*) Together, Cardinal Bernardin and Father Clements said a Mass for the opening of the new Holy Angels Church on June 9, 1991, exactly five years after the fire.

At an overnight gathering at Mundelein Seminary, Cardinal Bernardin
(*above, center*) meets with one hundred of the thousand diocesan priests of the
Archdiocese (one of a series of ten meetings) to discuss a wide range of topics.
During these meetings everyone is encouraged to express his own views.
The Cardinal takes copious notes and responds to all issues raised.

The Cardinal communicates on many levels. He speaks with his hands, punctuating his sentences with gestures that accentuate his message.

Cardinal Bernardin loves working with young people. Here he warms up a crowd of fifteen thousand teenagers before a Catholic Youth Office concert at the Rosemont Horizon in 1986. One of the Cardinal's trademarks is the way he bounces on his feet at high points in his speeches. Former students nicknamed him "Pepsi" for his effervescent speaking style.

5

The Shepherd

"I believe in the Lord, and I love Him with all my mind and heart and soul. The great desire of my life—a desire which intensifies as I grow older—is to be intimately united with Him, so that I can experience in the depth of my being His great love for me; so that I can allow His life to become my life.

"I also wish to affirm and encourage each of you as you search for the Lord and seek to grow in intimacy with Him. I ask you to join with me in prayer for all those who are not close to the Lord, for the many people who desperately need to experience His love, but have not placed themselves at His mercy. I am confident that Christ, the Good Shepherd, will answer our prayers."

[Most Reverend Joseph L. Bernardin, Homily for Liturgy of Solemn Installation of the Seventh Archbishop of Chicago, Holy Name Cathedral, August 25, 1982]

Cardinal Bernardin incenses the altar and crucifix during the celebration of Mass at Holy Name Cathedral.

Even an archbishop must enter the space of authority as one does a corrida, through a veil of acclaim and danger. Authority's arena was hardly smooth anywhere when Joseph Bernardin came to Chicago in 1982. Since the death of Mayor Richard J. Daley six years before, three mayors had served the city, three presidents had served the nation, and three popes had served the universal church. Did an authority figure still have a well-defined space to fill or was it now a gap into which he might easily fall?

As Rachel had grieved for her children so the Archdiocese grieved for the initiatives it thought lost and the energies smothered in the vacuum of Cardinal Cody's long autumnal decline. It had anticipated Bernardin's arrival as a deliverance and yet, in a church that at one moment wanted a patriarchal savior and, at another, valued a bishop according to "how much he left you alone," the challenge to the warmly received Bernardin was not small or simple. Crowds cheered matadors, he understood, but they were also ready for death in the afternoon.

The new shepherd was imbued with the ideals of the Second Vatican Council. If the church of Chicago were to draw its enormous strengths together, its members would have to work collegially, from the bottom up instead of in the once-presumed divinely inspired top-down manner. A *pastor* is "one who feeds," Bernardin knew, but a *bishop* is "one who sees." He would nourish his flock spiritually and provide the vision of a renewed church; he would also stand at their center at prayer and worship, but priests and people would themselves do the work of building a church for the coming century.

Although around his neck he wore the pallium, the thin wool band marked with five crosses that symbolized his official authority over Chicago's Catholics, the new shepherd did not invoke such potent symbols of office to command obedience. He remained himself and those who know him well observed that there was really no difference between the public leader and the private man. To be histrionic would have violated his good sense as well as his good nature. He might be so exact and thorough, so insistent on full preparation for every task that priests good-naturedly joked that he would not say grace at a banquet without a notecard, but his

extraordinary intelligence, his openness, and his genuineness caused people to pause and turn in his direction to hear what he had to say. He spoke as one having authority according to its root meaning in *augere*, "to increase, to make able to grow," rather than to control. People responded in accord with the root meaning of obedience, *ob-audire*, "to listen to," by freely giving him their attention.

The new Archbishop's calm and collaborative style, his self-possession even in the eye of hurricane pressures, also made him a shepherd to the shepherds, a natural leader among the nation's and the world's bishops. Cardinal Bernardin combined in himself the elements of authority and obedience, a commitment to the growth of others and an ability to listen to them. Although he appeared on the cover of *Time* magazine as the progressive leader who chaired the American Bishops' historic pastoral letter condemning the use of nuclear arms, he was regarded by everybody as a leader who could be trusted to take everybody's observations into account. It was Bernardin to whom they turned to untangle snarled problems or to

integrate fresh moral insights such as his "Consistent Ethic of Life" in which he broadened the base of the Pro-Life movement by connecting all the issues that underscored the value of human existence.

So, too, in Chicago, he raised hard questions in his gentle voice—questions that the priests and people had to answer together with him. These included the need to close or consolidate parishes or schools, the support of Catholic education in the inner city, the development of a process to deal with the tragic problems of sexual abuse that began to taint the clergy. Only a shepherd who believed deeply in God's work and in himself could remain, among his people as among his brother bishops, trustworthy through such frequently difficult explorations. Yet the dutiful, good-humored boy could still be seen within the world-acclaimed shepherd, the self-effacing leader who never forgot his origins and could laugh with a thousand banquet guests when the master of ceremonies said that success was not a surprise for the Archbishop: "His parents, after all, were named Mary and Joseph."

The Cardinal holds the crozier, which reflects the role of a bishop who gathers and shepherds the people of God. Here he blesses his flock during a Mass at Holy Name Cathedral.

(*Right*) Bernardin walks in procession at a solemn ceremony in the cathedral.

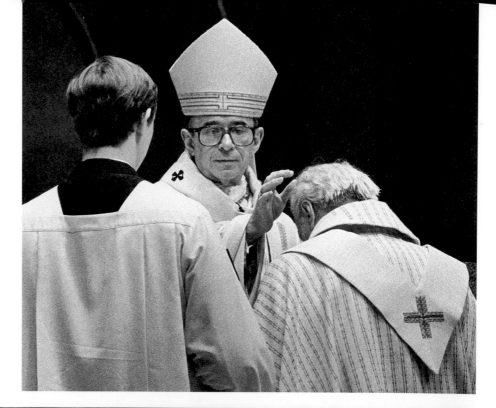

(*Top*) During the ordination of Thad J. Jakubowski and John R. Gorman as bishops in 1988, Cardinal Bernardin imposes hands on Bishop Jakubowski. This ancient gesture expresses the outpouring of the Holy Spirit and is the heart of the ordination rite.

(*Above*) The Cardinal then places the book of the Gospels over the head of the new bishop to demonstrate the power of the Word of God.

(*Right*) Bishops Jakubowski and Gorman prostrate themselves before the altar in preparation for episcopal ordination.

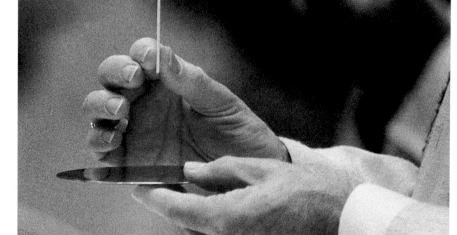

Hands of Worship.

(*Above left*) The Cardinal embraces the cross he wears during a service.

(*Above right*) Bernardin calls his people to prayer.

(*Right*) The Cardinal consecrates the Host during the celebration of Mass.

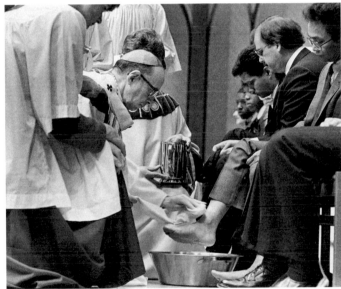

(*Above*) On Holy Thursday,
Cardinal Bernardin reenacts
Christ's humble gesture by
washing the feet of twelve of
his parishioners at Holy Name
Cathedral.

(*Left*) Cardinal Bernardin reads
the prayers during a Mass at the
cathedral.

(*Above and right*) Cardinal Bernardin presides at the funeral Mass for Monsignor James V. Murphy on December 20, 1985.

(*Following pages*) Like a light in the darkness, Cardinal Bernardin's life has provided guidance and direction to the faithful.

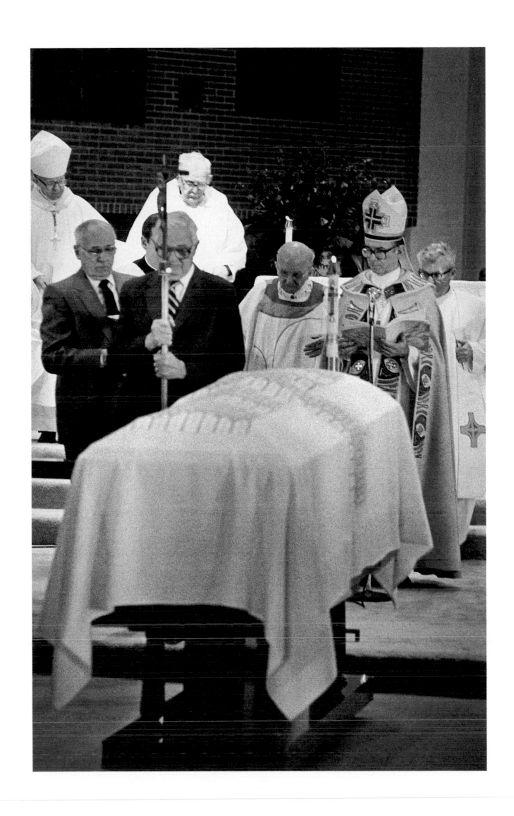

Cardinal Bernardin says the Lord's Prayer with parishioners of Saint Mark's Church. The Cardinal has always stressed the importance of strong community and fosters such togetherness by visiting as many parishes as possible each year.

(*Right*) Beneath the crucifix in the chapel of Little Sisters of the Poor, the Cardinal concludes Mass with a blessing.

(*Above*) Cardinal Bernardin notes that the rain has held out long enough for those celebrating their golden wedding anniversaries to enjoy an outdoor gathering on the steps of Holy Name Cathedral.

(*Left*) There are no barriers between Cardinal Bernardin and his people.

After the Mass, the Cardinal signs programs for those commemorating fifty years of marriage. An annual event, the golden anniversary Mass rekindles the spirit of love and commitment.

(*Top and above*) Cardinal Bernardin enjoys a student skit performed for him at Saint Rose Day School, 4911 South Hoyne Street.

(*Left*) Each year the Cardinal invites expectant mothers to a special Mass at Holy Name Cathedral. Here he offers a rose and his blessing to each soon-to-be mom.

The Cardinal celebrates Christmas Midnight Mass with his priests at Holy Name Cathedral.

(*Right*) Cardinal Bernardin discusses the Archdiocese with his friend Basil Cardinal Hume as they walk along the halls of Mundelein Seminary.

The visitor arrived with a smile and left with a bouquet of roses. The sisters at Saint Rose school watch the Cardinal depart with a blooming souvenir of his visit there.

6
Agony and Triumph

"I see the last two years [1993–1995] as a significant period, a kind of trinity of events. First the accusation of sex abuse, then Steven Cook's recantation and our reconciliation, then this cancer diagnosis. . . .

"It is striking that most people connect these two incidents. Journalists ask me which of the two was worse, the false accusation or the cancer. I tell them that the accusation of sex abuse was worse. When it came out and the news immediately went around the world, I was helpless, in a sense, and felt completely vulnerable, left to rely completely on myself.

"The news of cancer was completely different. It is a natural thing that we are all subject to illness, that we all have to die. Illness, even when it has the prospect of death, is very different from a false accusation.

"My faith is the source of my confidence. . . . A person's outlook would be very different without faith. . . . In my 43 years as a priest I have always encouraged people to rely on their faith in bad times. . . . I'm just putting into practice what I've always preached."

[Joseph Cardinal Bernardin, *Notre Dame Magazine*, Autumn 1995]

Alone with the Lord. Cardinal Bernardin withdraws for a private moment in the midst of an anniversary Mass at Saint Joseph's Church in Wilmette. This was one of the first major services he attended after having cancer surgery.

Space wears mystery as the year does its seasons, immersed in time as well as distance. These aspects of space interpenetrate on the important occasions of our lives, each seeding us with its own special signals so that they are married in remembrance and seem as inseparable as the sounds of a symphony. How *long* has it been since childhood, we ask, because it seems so *far* away?

Space and time tighten at Thanksgiving. We feel life and death in our bones as the days bend before winter as trees before a storm, growing shorter and moving faster. In the tension of such a November in 1993, a mystery passing all these enveloped Joseph Cardinal Bernardin, stopping time and leaving him alone in a desert vast space. A few days before the nation's Catholic bishops were to convene in Washington, D.C., Bernardin was accused of having sexually abused a former Cincinnati seminarian almost twenty years before while he was Archbishop there.

Nor did the charge lack the devil's own malice. No lonelier place exists than the dock in which the innocent stand blinded by the klieg lights of false accusation. Before Cardinal Bernardin could read the allegations, they were broadcast throughout the world. It quickly became clear that the lawyer who initiated the case had offered the Cable News Network an exclusive preview of the charges. Provided with a look at the supposed evidence and interviews with the accuser, Steven Cook, the network aired an exclusive program on the situation on the Sunday before the opening of the bishops' meeting.

On the Thursday before the CNN broadcast, rumors circulated that formal charges would be filed the next day. Most Chicagoans rejected the charges against the man they had come to know so well, and they embraced him, whether in the passing truck driver's thumbs-up signal or in the standing ovations he received in every parish. Nonetheless, despite the advice of many advisors, he was ultimately alone in dealing with the rumors of reporters waiting restlessly to question him the next high noon, he spent some time by himself in his office, thinking of how he had lived and worked and of how he should face this most harrowing test of all his days. He called a friend and told him his decision, "I'm going to handle this on my own. I'm going to answer every question and tell the truth. If my advisors don't agree, they can go their own way."

Bernardin stepped into the noisy glare, the shouted questions of almost one hundred journalists, and answered every inquiry simply and directly as he would to another media gathering a few days later in Washington, D.C. And something happened in that noisy room: it suddenly grew quiet as the Cardinal spoke. The bindings on the rack of time and space loosened and fell away, their pressures dissolved in that space by the power of truth and a transparently good man. The reporters had eagerly assembled to get a good story but found instead a good man. They, rather than the Cardinal, were changed by the experience. By being undefended, Bernardin had disarmed the professionals whose ordinary work was the pursuit of sin not the discovery of virtue.

It was in the days of the least light of the next winter that Cardinal Bernardin made a pilgrimage to Philadelphia to effect a reconciliation with his dying accuser who, ten months before, had admitted that his accusations had been false. Before spring arrived in 1994, Bernardin was exonerated as publicly as he had been indicted. Yet no space of his life had gone unexamined during the months during which the structure of false accusation collapsed in on itself like a dynamited building. Bernardin's own truth had made him free, opening up the space of his life again. Yet, for him as a priest, it was the now heavily shadowed space of Steven Cook's life he wanted to enter, to give him the bread of peace and the wine of faith for the journey into the mystery that lay just ahead.

Hours after sexual abuse charges were filed against him in 1993, Cardinal Bernardin calmly faced a throng of reporters packed into an office at the archdiocesan headquarters. Thirty-four-year-old Steven J. Cook filed the lawsuit claiming that Bernardin, then the Archbishop of Cincinnati, had sexually abused him when he was a teenage seminary student there. Despite the pain of facing an accusation that Cook eventually recanted, Bernardin greeted the public with his typical smile.

(*Top left*) In the glare of TV lights, Cardinal Bernardin answered reporters' questions about the lawsuit. "Everything that is in that suit about me is totally untrue, totally false," he declared. "I am sixty-five years old, and I can tell you that all my life I have lived a chaste and celibate life. . . . In the final analysis, I am not really concerned about myself. I know that I am innocent. I'm more concerned about my people, the people whom I love, the people whom I shepherd."

(*Bottom left*) At the end of his press conference, Cardinal Bernardin smiled graciously as he walked out of the spotlights. Already that day he had forwarded a copy of the allegations to a fitness review board that examines allegations of sexual misconduct by priests. The review board had been established by the Cardinal himself the year before. By the following spring, Cook, suffering from AIDS, recanted his allegations. Ten months later, Cardinal Bernardin flew to Philadelphia to meet with Cook. The Cardinal, who had been praying for Cook's health and peace of mind all along, told the dying man that he harbored no ill feelings toward him. Cook apologized for the pain and embarrassment he had caused. After their talk, Bernardin celebrated Mass for Cook, who died of complications from AIDS one year later.

(*Above*) The front-page headline of the March 1, 1994, *Chicago Sun-Times* confirmed what Bernardin's flock had believed all along.

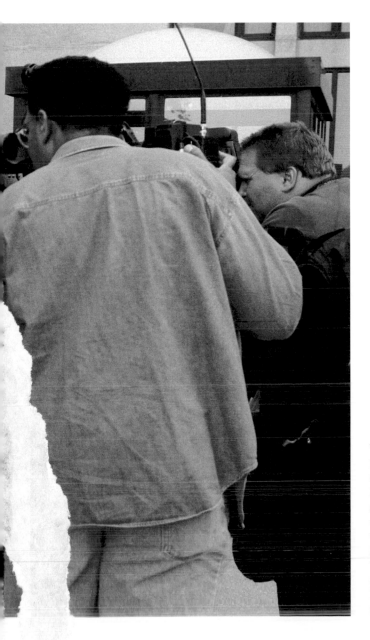

With the pain of false accusation starting to subside, Cardinal Bernardin turned the corner only to come face-to-face with the second greatest trial of his life in as many years: cancer. Doctors determined that growths on the Cardinal's pancreas and right kidney warranted exploratory surgery. Sunday evening, June 11, 1995, the Cardinal met reporters and well-wishers outside Loyola University Medical Center in Maywood, Illinois, as he checked in and prepared for the 7:40 A.M. surgery the next morning. A longtime friend and confidant, Father Kenneth Velo, and the Cardinal's sister, Elaine Addison (*top*), watched as the Cardinal took time to respond to reporters' questions about his condition (*left*).

On Monday, June 12, 1995, the day of Cardinal Bernardin's surgery, anxious Chicagoans awaited news of the Cardinal's status as local TV stations aired frequent updates. Dr. Warren Furey, Bernardin's personal physician, informed viewers that the Cardinal was in good hands. Dr. Gerard Aranha, the chief surgeon from Loyola University Medical Center, was in charge of the seven-hour procedure. Bishop Raymond Goedert, the Vicar General, took charge of the Archdiocese during this critical period.

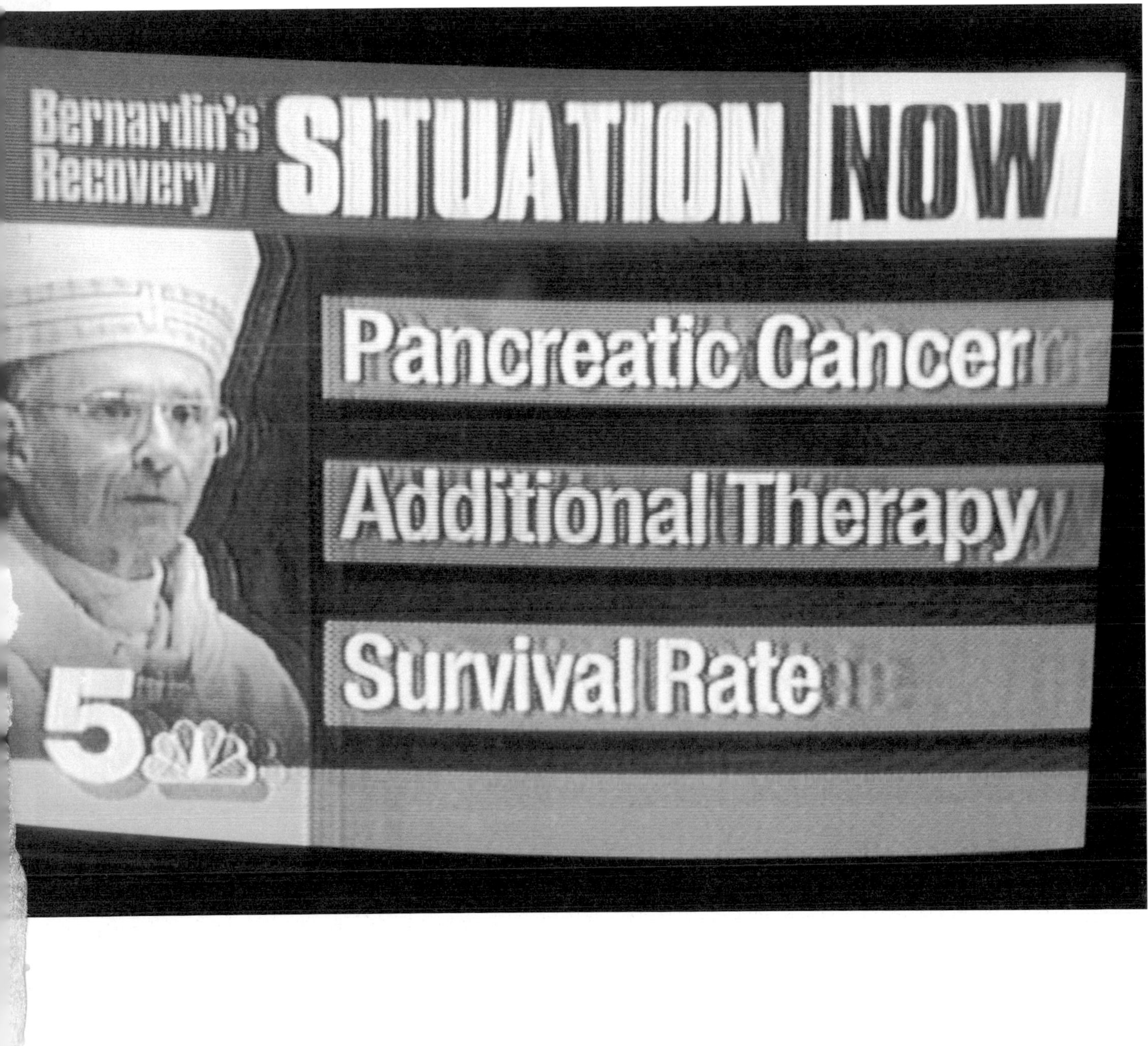
Bernardin's Recovery
SITUATION NOW
Pancreatic Cancer
Additional Therapy
Survival Rate
5

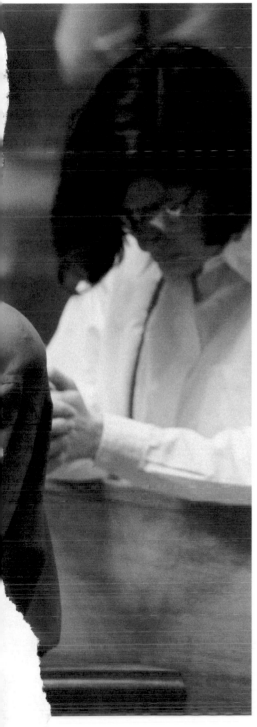

All across the city people prayed for the Cardinal. The pews at Holy Name Cathedral were filled. (*Left*) Joan Walker and her son offer prayers for their Archbishop. (*Above, from left to right*) Mary Hallan, F. Octavie Mosimann, and Sister Mary Lucia Skalka pray for their friend.

The day before his surgery, the Cardinal had received many phone calls and words of support. One of those calls came from Pope John Paul II, another from Steven Cook, the man who had falsely accused the Cardinal nineteen months earlier.

On the morning of the Cardinal's surgery, a seagull soared through the sky above Lake Michigan. The sky spoke that morning. It represented light and darkness, joy and pain, sickness and health. The seagull flew with great strength and great courage until it became part of the sky. There was peace.

Six days after surgery, Cardinal Bernardin called John H. White to take the first picture of him since being admitted to Loyola University Medical Center. With the Cardinal is Sister Mary Brian Costello, RSM, his chief of staff. The Cardinal is holding a letter from eleven-year-old Kelly Noone, asking him to pray for her grandfather, Jim Regan, who was a patient two doors down the hall.

Dear Cardinal Bernaldin,
I really hope you get better as soon as possible. You are in my prayers. ☺ Guess What? Last Wednesday my grandfather was very sick (he was two doors down from where you were staying) and when you came on the floor a couple days later he got 110% better WOW!! Right now he is doing very good! 🙂 I heard on the news that you were walking around the halls (THAT'S GREAT!) and I was just wondering if you ever had a chance could you come in and please bless my grandpa he is in room # ~~600~~ 6301 His name is Jim Regan. My name is Kelly Noone.

At the end of an intense twenty-eight-day cycle of chemotherapy and radiation treatments, the Cardinal made a surprisingly long appearance at a picnic hosted in the backyard of his residence. None of the young people attending the "Theology on Tap" picnic expected to see their recovering leader, but he greeted every one of his guests in the pleasant summer afternoon.

Six weeks later, on September 25, 1995, Cardinal Bernardin returned to his priestly duties. Like a professional athlete suiting up for an important game, he put on his vestments to conduct a special prayer service for the priests of the Archdiocese at Holy Name Cathedral.

(*Left*) The Cardinal reviews his homily before beginning the service with his priests.

(*Below*) During the service he shared a message he has consistently delivered throughout his life: "My best gift to you is *myself*. Beneath the titles of archbishop or cardinal is a man, Joseph Bernardin, . . . of great faith, one who is in love with the Lord, one who struggles each day—sometimes with little obvious success—to decrease so the Lord can increase in him, a man whose life is full of crooked lines but who is willing to let the Lord write straight with them. . . . Know that this man, Joseph, loves you . . ."

Praying with the priests of the Archdiocese after cancer surgery was a highly emotional event. Nearly five hundred priests attended. "We all felt it was very important to pray together," Cardinal Bernardin says. "At that point I was eager to get back to my ministerial duties and to continue with my work. I am continually thankful for the great support and love my fellow priests share with me and the Archdiocese."

7
Moving Forward

"When I entered the Loyola University Medical Center last June [1995], my life had been turned completely upside down by the totally unexpected news that what I had been experiencing as a healthy body was, in fact, housing a dangerous, aggressive cancer. The time since the diagnosis, surgery, and postoperative radiation and chemotherapy has lead me into a new dimension of my lifelong journey of faith.

". . . I came to believe in a new way that the Lord would walk with me through this journey of illness that would take me from a former way of life into a new manner of living.

"Nevertheless, during my convalescence I found the nights to be especially long, a time for various fears to surface. I sometimes found myself weeping, something I seldom did before. And I came to realize how much of what consumes our daily life truly is trivial and insignificant. In these dark moments, besides my faith and trust in the Lord, I was constantly bolstered by the awareness that thousands of people were praying for me throughout the Archdiocese, and, indeed, the world. I have been graced by an outpouring of affection and support that has allowed me to experience ecclesial life as a 'community of hope' in a very intimate way.

"I have also felt a special solidarity with others facing life-threatening illness. I have talked and prayed with other cancer patients who were waiting in the same room for radiation or chemotherapy. I have been contacted by hundreds of people seeking my advice and prayers on behalf of family or friends suffering a serious illness, often cancer."

[Joseph Cardinal Bernardin, "A Sign of Hope," A Pastoral Letter on Healthcare, October 18, 1995]

Cardinal Bernardin rests his hand on eight-year-old Gabriela Mejia's head and prays for her health during a visit to Children's Memorial Hospital in Chicago at the end of 1995.

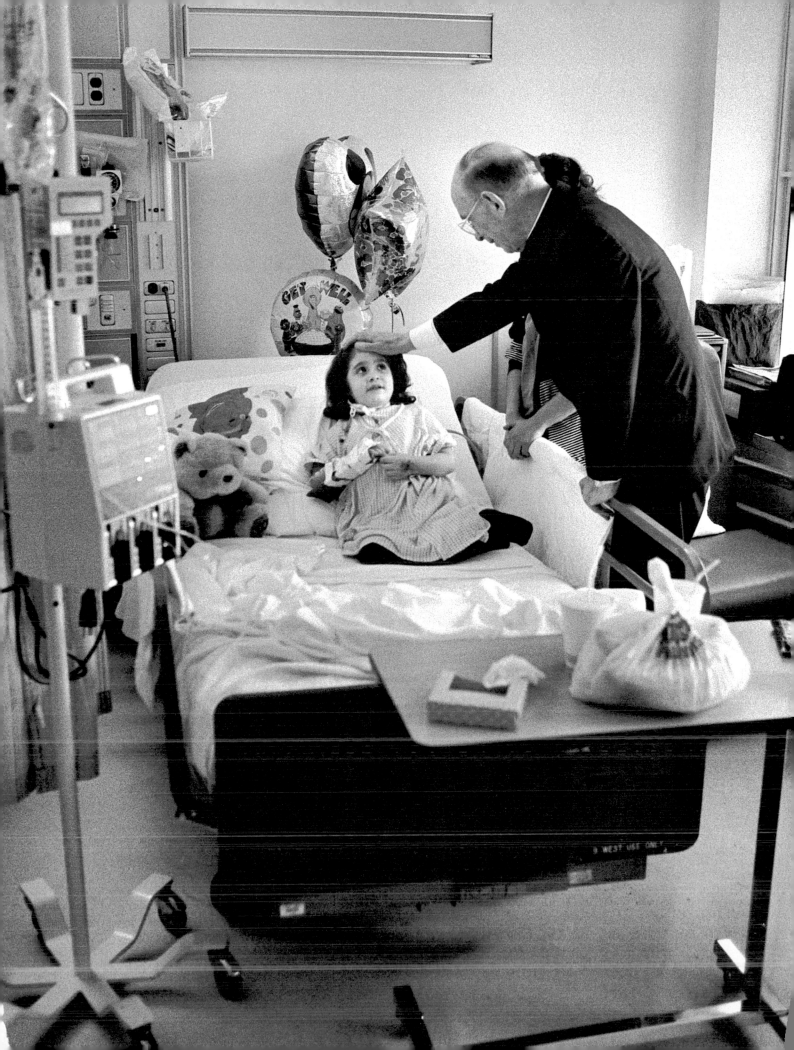

As near-summer sunlight stretched like a dancer across the city, the place Cardinal Bernardin occupied in Chicago became clear to everybody. That place was not their minds, filled now with full knowledge of him, or that portion of attention that pays respect to dignitaries. As the story that the Archbishop had been stricken with pancreatic cancer broke like war news, people realized that their archbishop had quietly moved into the space of their hearts.

He had entered there as the Dolomite-born streams did the land of his parents, gently, naturally, nourishing rather than depleting the earth, bearing refreshment for everybody. Now, as diocesan officials gravely watched his physicians describe the forthcoming surgery on a televised news conference, Chicagoans knew that they did not just admire, or like, but loved Cardinal Bernardin.

They wanted to stand with him but they knew that, once again, Bernardin had to make pilgrimage alone into the innermost chambers of mystery. It seemed neither right nor comprehensible that the just-cleared path of his life should now suddenly narrow and lead him, beyond their sight or calling out, into the Valley of the Shadow of Death itself.

Standing at the center of this new mystery, the Cardinal prepared for his surgery by calming the families around him: his sister, Elaine, and her children and the relatives beyond counting in Italy; the official family of the Archdiocese by systematically delegating his duties to his assistant bishops; the extended family of Chicago, praying anxiously now that he be restored to full health. They could see him better on that weekend before he entered Loyola University Medical Center as he spoke to reporters of his need for the kind of faith he had preached to others about all his life. Ordinary men and women knew that they loved him because of his instinctive feeling for everything human and because, for him, religion's purpose lay more in helping people get up than in making them feel guilty for falling down in the first place.

Barely two months later, recovering in his residence, Cardinal Bernardin spoke of the passage from which he had returned no less a Cardinal Archbishop but more of a priest.

"I've become unofficial chaplain to all the seriously ill people, especially those with cancer, in the metropolitan area," he says, pointing to the letters, speaking of the phone calls, telling especially of his fellow patients, young and old, or of the strangers who speak to him when he is at the hospital for treatment. The enormously moving character of his new role is compressed in one anecdote of a man who gave his wallet picture of his dying wife to the Cardinal and asked him to keep it "to remember her and to pray for her." He pauses before he speaks, "These are the people I want to spend my time with now."

He tells of one of his own doctors asking him to see a woman who was very frightened by her illness. "She began to see things differently when I told her that I know fear very well myself. I feel it, I told her, when I wake up in the middle of the night and it seems that I am very alone with this. That kind of fear is part of our being human." He speaks of a conviction that he never lost but that he now looks at freshly: Such simple encounters, beyond administration, building, or holding meetings, lie at the heart of a priest's life and work.

Even if not specifically religious, says Cardinal Bernardin, "men and women everywhere have a deep desire to come in contact with the transcendent. The clergy can be a symbol of that, the medium for that by the simple goodness they show in being with their people. *That's* what ordinary people want. I believe that with all my heart. The things they remember most are small acts of concern and thoughtfulness. Years later, *that* is what they tell you about their priests, not about the big drives but the little kindnesses. We would be better served if people could see right through us."

"*Consistency*," he answers when asked of an important quality for priests. "Sometimes in life, people seem to change. Others say of them 'They are not the person I once knew.'" He looks up, unbowed, ready for the next challenge. His trials have made Cardinal Bernardin so transparent that people easily see his simple goodness. "I'm glad," he says softly, unself-consciously, innocently, "when people tell me that I'm the same Joe Bernardin they have known for forty years."

Besides writing letters and making phone calls to those who are seriously ill, the Cardinal visits patients in hospitals throughout Chicago. During a visit in December of 1995 to Children's Memorial Hospital, Bernardin spent time with nine-day-old Jakwanna Desiree Grant and her mother, Adrienne (*right*); smiled at one-month-old Zachary Tomas Davila while his mother, Joellyn Robinson, read from a storybook (*bottom right*); and offered comforting words to Edwin Fuentes as he prayed for his son Angel's recovery (*below*).

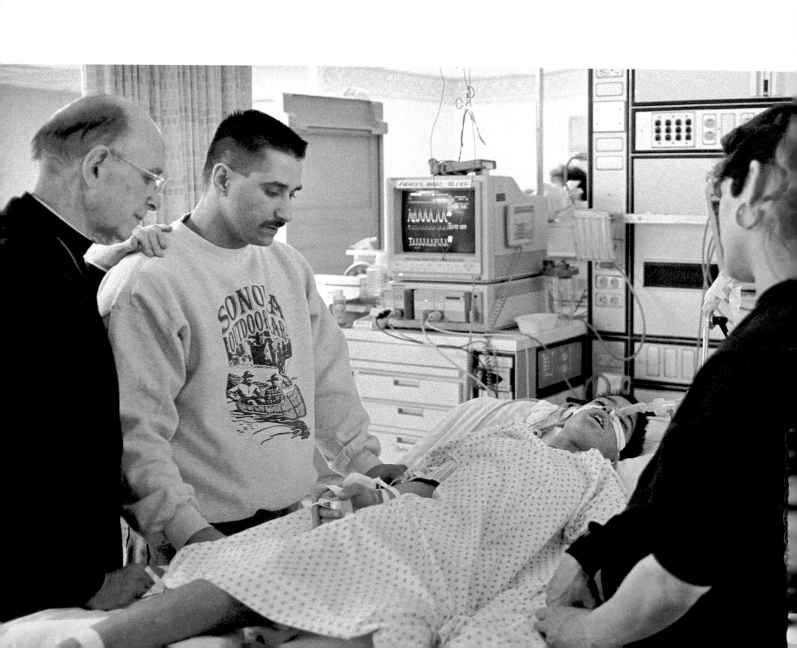

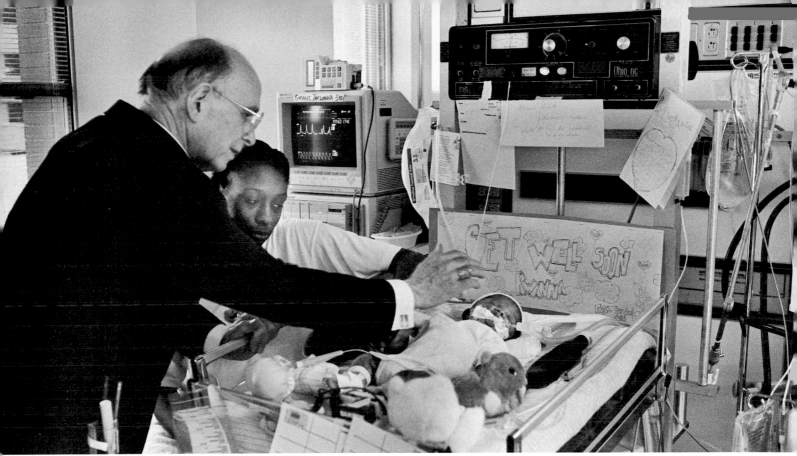

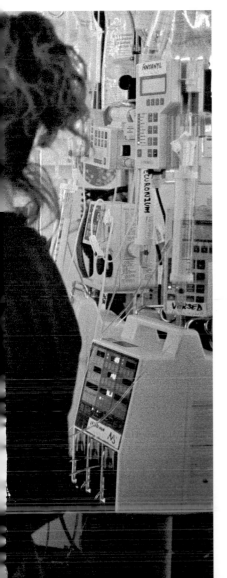

The Cardinal limited his work schedule through December following his surgery, but he did find strength to attend special functions. The 150th anniversary of Saint Joseph's Church in Wilmette on November 26, 1995, was one such event.

(*Above*) The Cardinal walks with Father Francis Kane, the pastor of Saint Joseph's.

(*Left*) Ninety-five-year-old Anna Bosshart shared in the excitement.

(*Far left*) During the celebration Bernardin greeted four-year-old Courtney Kuhnen as her mother, Candice Kuhnen (*standing right*), looked on.

(*Following pages*) Greeting the Pope. Cardinal Bernardin, in high spirits after a tough five months, awaits the Pontiff as plainclothes agents handle crowd control.

Pope John Paul II landed at Newark, New Jersey, October 4, 1995, to begin a five-day visit to the United States. As he descended the steps of his Alitalia jetliner, "Shepherd One," the Pope reached out his hand to acknowledge a steady drizzle that fell on the crowd of welcomers waiting patiently on the tarmac.

Among those waiting to greet the Pope were President Bill Clinton and First Lady Hillary Rodham Clinton, several Catholic members of the Cabinet, and a delegation of cardinals. Cardinal Bernardin is third from the end of the greeting line.

Cardinal Bernardin and his friends James Cardinal Hickey (*far left*) and Bernard Cardinal Law brave the wind and rain as they wait for the Pope to make his way through the welcoming line.

(*Right*) The Holy Father and Cardinal Bernardin were glad to see each other. After learning that his friend's surgery had gone well and that the prognosis looked good, the Pope said "Thanks be to God" and assured the Cardinal of his continued prayers.

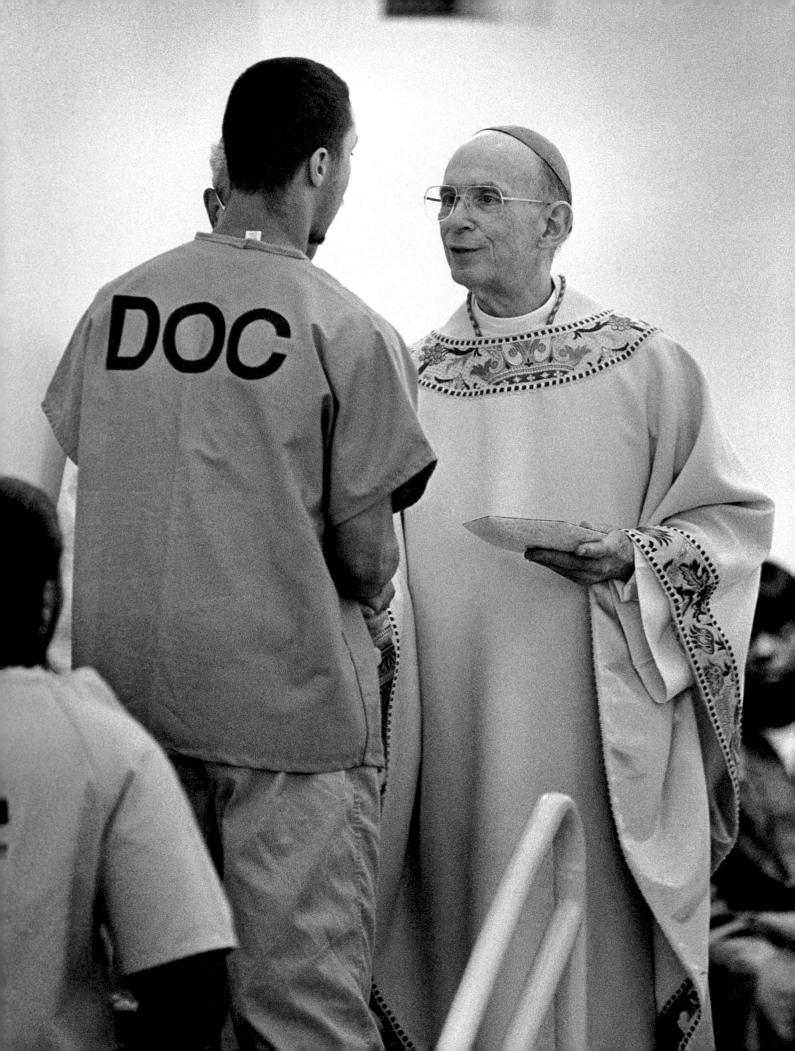

Each year Cardinal Bernardin celebrates Christmas Mass at the Cook County Correctional Facility for worshippers dressed in uniforms marked DOC—for Department of Corrections. "I come as a friend, a brother, who respects and loves you," said the Cardinal in his 1995 homily. "I am not here to judge you; neither is it within my power to set you free. But I can give you another kind of freedom—the freedom that comes from being at peace with God, knowing that he loves us and will stand with us through life's trials.

"... I know this inner peace from personal experience. Last June, when my doctors discovered that I had an aggressive cancer, the worst fears of my life suddenly became a reality. . . . Why do I share this with you this morning? Because I want you to know that from the very beginning of this illness I placed my life totally in God's hands, confident of his abiding love for me. And because of this I have experienced the deepest inner peace I have ever known.

"My dear brothers and sisters, I urge you this morning to place your lives in God's hands, confident that his love for you is abiding."

While many people were busy opening Christmas gifts, Cardinal Bernardin was leaving the jail, his mission accomplished.

169

At Sacred Heart Church in suburban Palos Hills, Cardinal Bernardin celebrated the final Simbang Gabi Mass, a Philippine tradition of nine consecutive evenings of Advent Masses in preparation for Christmas. In attendance were members of thirty-four parishes of the Filipino community. Young people are an important part of the Mass. One child, dressed as an angel (*top right*), was responsible for taking the gifts to the altar. During the Mass, Cardinal Bernardin administered Holy Communion to Edward Bulow III (*right*), a young man suffering from cancer.

(*Right*) Cardinal Bernardin in his bedroom. On the dresser is a picture of his late father, Joseph.

(*Below*) On Christmas Day 1995, Cardinal Bernardin visited his mother, Maria, at her residence at Little Sisters of the Poor. They posed for their annual Christmas photograph. Now ninety-one, Maria enjoyed talking with her son and their friend Sister Marcel Joseph. During the visit Sister Marcel asked Maria how she felt. Maria responded, "I'm so full of love, and I want to share it with everybody."

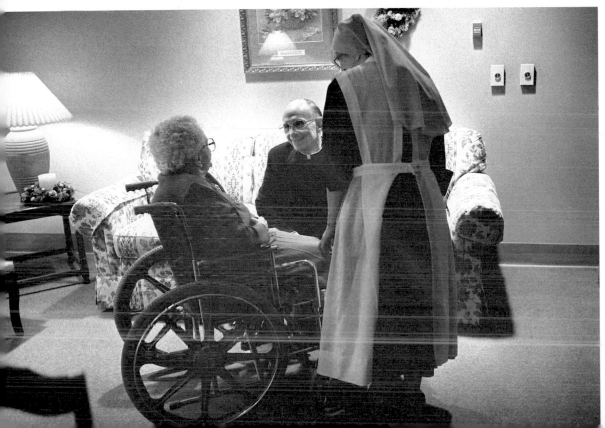

The circle of life. At the end of 1995 Cardinal Bernardin baptized five-month-old Nora Jane Ya McGuffey in a small chapel in Holy Name Cathedral. The baby, who was born in China and adopted by Margie and Tom McGuffey, rested in the arms of her godmother, Jeanne McGuffey. The baptismal dress worn by Nora Jane has been in Margie's family for more than one hundred years.

Bearing his own cross. As Joseph Cardinal Bernardin undergoes weekly chemotherapy treatments to keep the cancer from returning, he is realistic about his illness. Doctors have given the Cardinal a 20 to 25 percent chance to survive the next five years. Joseph Bernardin continues to embrace life with a deep love of God and God's people. Never far from his mind are the words he spoke at Holy Name Cathedral during his installation as Chicago's Archbishop: "For however many years I am given, I give myself to you. I offer you my service and leadership, my energies, my gifts, my mind, my heart, my strength, and yes, my limitations. I offer you myself in faith, hope, and love."

After a long and moving 1995 Christmas Midnight Mass
at Little Sisters of the Poor, Cardinal Bernardin shared
the benediction with his people.

"May Almighty God bless you, the Father and the
Son and the Holy Spirit. Go in peace to love and
serve the Lord. Amen."

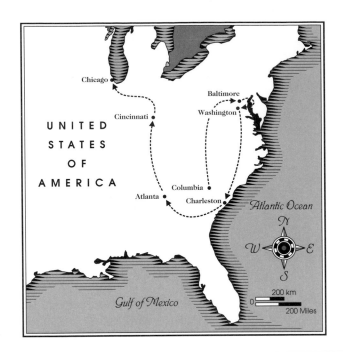

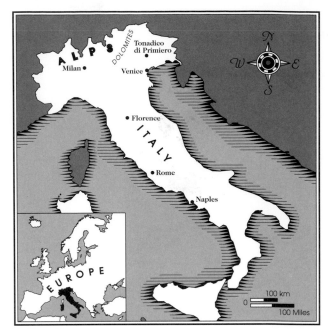

Key Dates in the Life of Joseph Cardinal Bernardin

April 2, 1928	Joseph Louis Bernardin was born in Columbia, South Carolina, to Joseph and Maria M. Simion Bernardin. After attending Catholic and public schools and the University of South Carolina, Bernardin was accepted as a candidate for the priesthood. He studied at Saint Mary's College in Kentucky; Saint Mary's Seminary in Baltimore, where he received a Bachelor of Arts degree in philosophy; and at the Catholic University of America in Washington, D.C., where in 1951 he received a Master of Arts degree in Education.
April 26, 1952	Ordained to the priesthood for the Diocese of Charleston at Saint Joseph Church, Columbia, South Carolina. During his fourteen years in the Diocese of Charleston, he served in many capacities under four bishops.
1959	Named a papal chamberlain.
1962	Named a domestic prelate by Pope John XXIII.
March 9, 1966	Appointed Auxiliary Bishop of Atlanta by Pope Paul VI. Upon his appointment he became the youngest bishop in the country.
April 10, 1968	Elected General Secretary of the National Conference of Catholic Bishops and the United States Catholic Conference.
November 21, 1972	Appointed Archbishop of Cincinnati by Pope Paul VI. He served the Ohio Metropolitan See for almost ten years.
November 1974	Elected to a three-year term as president of the National Conference of Catholic Bishops and United States Catholic Conference. He served until 1977.
July 10, 1982	Appointed Archbishop of Chicago by Pope John Paul II.
August 25, 1982	Installed as Archbishop of Chicago in ceremonies at Holy Name Cathedral.
February 2, 1983	Elevated to the College of Cardinals by Pope John Paul II.
December 1983	Introduced concept of Consistent Ethic of Life (at Fordham University).
1986	Established Big Shoulders Fund to support inner-city Catholic schools.
1991	Celebrated twenty-fifth anniversary as bishop.
March 1994	Vindicated of charges of sexual abuse.
March 1995	Made first pilgrimage to the Holy Land with delegation of Catholic and Jewish leaders from Chicago.
June 1995	Underwent cancer surgery at Loyola University Medical Center.
April 2, 1996	"Cancer-free" Cardinal Bernardin celebrated his sixty-eighth birthday.